4

Zaner-Bloser
Handwriting

ZB Zaner-Bloser

Credits

Art: Shel Silverstein: 6, 108; John Hovell: 15–17, 47, 92, 93, 94, 95, 103; Gary Krejca/Wilkinson Studios: 57, 67; Tom Leonard: 92

Literature: "It's Dark in Here" from *Where the Sidewalk Ends* by Shel Silverstein. Copyright © 1974 by Evil Eye Music, Inc.

Photos: moodboard/Corbis: Cover; ©iStockphoto.com/stepanjezek: 4, 36; ©iStockphoto.com/EcoPic: 4, 42; ©iStockphoto.com/jasantiso: 4, 63; George C. Anderson Photography, Inc.: 5, 10–14, 17, 18, 50; ©Corbis/Getty Images: 24; ©iStockphoto.com/asterix0597: 25; ©iStockphoto.com/kassandra: 31; ©iStockphoto.com/stephenmeese: 37 (jaguar); ©iStockphoto.com/stephenmeese: 37 (toucan); ©iStockphoto.com/sacco: 37 (anaconda); ©Juice Images/Alamy: 38; ©Mauritius/SuperStock: 43; ©David Young-Wolff/PhotoEdit Inc.: 44; ©Henry Brown/Alamy: 56; ©Russell Burden/Photolibrary: 62; ©Jim Wehtje/Getty Images: 66; ©louis wulff/Alamy: 70; ©Comstock/Jupiterimages: 74; ©ASSOCIATED PRESS: 76; ©MARKA/Alamy: 85; ©iStockphoto.com/mpruitt: 86; ©Mark Polott/Photolibrary: 88; ©iStockphoto.com/Bluberries: 104; ©Gordon McGregor/Alamy: 106

ISBN: 978-1-4531-1799-6

Copyright © 2016 Zaner-Bloser, Inc.

ZB Code 16

Zaner-Bloser, Inc.
1-800-421-3018
www.zaner-bloser.com
Printed in the United States of America   3 4 5 6 7 8 9 10 11 997 21 20 19 18 17 16

SUSTAINABLE FORESTRY INITIATIVE Certified Sourcing www.sfiprogram.org SFI-01042

CONTENTS

Unit 4 Using What You Have Learned

Dear Principal Martin,

The Fourth Grade Recycling Project is in its second week. We have collected 52 pounds of newspaper and 310 aluminum cans!

As you requested, we will make a graph to show our results at the end of the project.

Sincerely,

Mrs. Rivera's Fourth Grade Class

You write for many reasons at school, at home, and in your community. The lessons in this book will help you write legibly so you and other people can easily read what you have written.

Handwriting Tutor

Scan the **Handwriting Tutor** codes with a mobile device to watch handwriting videos.

Stop and Check

Evaluating your own handwriting is a good habit to form. When you see the **Stop and Check** sign in this book, stop and circle the best letter you wrote on that line.

Handwriting Tutor

Keys to Legibility

Slant
Spacing
Size
Shape

You will see the **Keys to Legibility** throughout this book. They will help you remember to check the **Shape, Size, Spacing,** and **Slant** of your writing to make sure it is easy to read.

Handwriting Tutor

It's Dark in Here

I am writing these poems
From inside a lion,
And it's rather dark in here.
So please excuse the handwriting
Which may not be too clear.
But this afternoon by the lion's cage
I'm afraid I got too near.
And I'm writing these lines
From inside a lion,
And it's rather dark in here.

by Shel Silverstein

Write the poem in your best cursive handwriting. Remember to leave space for margins.

Is your writing easy to read?   Yes   No

Write your five best cursive letters.

Write five cursive letters you would like to improve.

Manuscript Letters and Numerals

Aa Bb Cc Dd Ee Ff Gg

Hh Ii Jj Kk Ll Mm Nn

Oo Pp Qq Rr Ss Tt Uu

Vv Ww Xx Yy Zz

1 2 3 4 5 6 7 8 9 10

Although most of your writing will be in cursive, you will still use manuscript for such things as address books, labels, and signs. Use your best manuscript to write the following.

1. Write your name.

_____

- - - - - - - - - - - - - - - - - - - -

_____

3. Write your initials and a friend's initials.

_____

- - - - - - - - - - - - - - - - - - - -

_____

2. Write a friend's name.

_____

- - - - - - - - - - - - - - - - - - - -

_____

4. Write your state abbreviation and ZIP code.

_____

- - - - - - - - - - - - - - - - - - - -

_____

Use one of the following ideas. Use manuscript to write a sign for your classroom door.

Come In   Please Knock   Welcome   Testing

Cursive Letters and Numerals

Aa Bb Cc Dd Ee Ff Gg
Hh Ii Jj Kk Ll Mm
Nn Oo Pp Qq Rr Ss Tt
Uu Vv Ww Xx Yy Zz
1 2 3 4 5 6 7 8 9 10

Use your best cursive to write the following.

1. Write your name.

_____

2. Write the name of your school.

_____

3. Write the numerals from 1 to 10.

_____

4. Write the lowercase letters you think you use most.

_____

5. Write the letters and numerals you want to improve.

_____

Left-Handed Writers

Sit like this.
Sit comfortably.
Lean forward a little.
Keep your feet flat on the floor.

Handwriting Tutor

Place the paper like this.

Handwriting Tutor

Slant the paper as shown in the picture.

Rest both arms on the desk. Use your right hand to shift the paper as you write.

Pull the pencil toward your left elbow when you write.

Hold the pencil like this.

Handwriting Tutor

Hold the pencil with your thumb and first two fingers.

Keep your first finger on top.

Bend your thumb and keep it on the side.

Do not squeeze the pencil when you write.

Right-Handed Writers

Sit like this.

Sit comfortably.

Lean forward a little.

Keep your feet flat on the floor.

 Handwriting Tutor

Place the paper like this.

 Handwriting Tutor

Slant the paper as shown in the picture.

Rest both arms on the desk. Use your left hand to shift the paper as you write.

Pull the pencil toward the middle of your body when you write.

Hold the pencil like this.

 Handwriting Tutor

Hold the pencil with your thumb and first two fingers.

Keep your first finger on top.

Bend your thumb and keep it on the side.

Do not squeeze the pencil when you write.

Undercurve

An **undercurve** is one of the basic strokes used to write cursive letters. An undercurve stroke swings up.

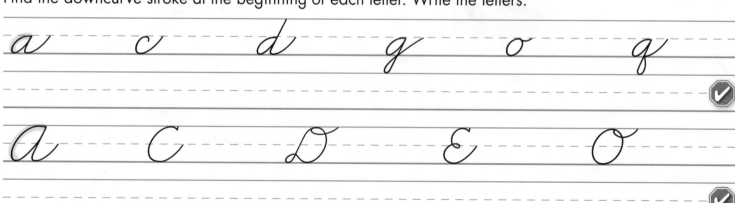

Find an undercurve stroke at the beginning of each letter. Write the letters.

b   e   h   j   p   t   w

B   G   L   P   R   S

Downcurve

A **downcurve** is one of the basic strokes used to write cursive letters. A downcurve stroke dives down.

Find the downcurve stroke at the beginning of each letter. Write the letters.

a   c   d   g   o   q

A   C   D   E   O

Overcurve

An **overcurve** is one of the basic strokes used to write cursive letters. An overcurve stroke bounces up.

Find the overcurve stroke at the beginning of each letter. Write the letters.

m   n   v   x   y   z

I   J   Q

Slant

A **slant** is one of the basic strokes used to write cursive letters. A slant stroke slides.

Find the slant stroke in each letter. Write the letters.

a   d   g   i   j   m   y

A   B   K   R   U   X   Y

Keys to Legibility

Handwriting Tutor

Make your writing easy to read.
As you write in cursive, pay attention
to the shape of your writing.

Shape

There are four basic strokes in cursive writing.
Be sure to write each letter with good basic strokes.

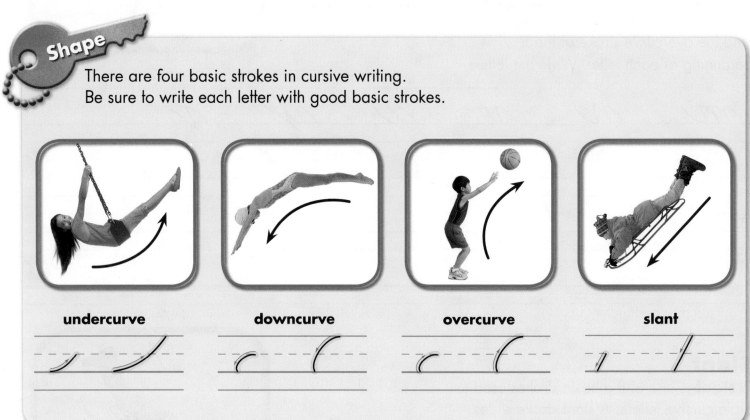

undercurve   **downcurve**   **overcurve**   **slant**

Write letters with undercurve strokes.

i   b   G   S

Write letters with downcurve strokes.

a   d   C   O

Write letters with overcurve strokes.

m   v   x   Q

Write letters with slant strokes.

t   p   B   R

14

Make your writing easy to read.
As you write in cursive, pay attention
to the size of your writing.

Size

Use the guidelines to help you make each letter the correct size.

Tall letters touch the headline.
All uppercase letters are tall.

b   A   h

Short letters touch the midline.

a   m   g   u

Some letters have descenders
that go below the baseline and
touch the next headline.

f   g   y

Write the tall letters.

d   h   l   t   E   G   F   n

Write the short letters.

a   e   i   o   m   a   v   x

Write the letters that have descenders.

g   j   f   q   z   z   f   Y

15

Keys to Legibility

Slant

Spacing

Size

Shape

Handwriting Tutor

Make your writing easy to read.
As you write in cursive, pay attention
to the spacing of your writing.

Spacing

Between Letters There should be enough space for O.

handwriting

Between Words There should be enough space for \.

between words

Between Sentences There should be enough space for O.

*Spacing is important. So
are shape and size.*

Write the sentences. Use correct spacing between letters, words, and sentences.

*My writing is neat. It
has good spacing.*

Make your writing easy to read. As you write in cursive, pay attention to the slant of your writing.

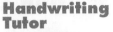

Slant

Cursive letters have a uniform forward slant.

forward slant

To write with good slant:

POSITION PULL SHIFT

- Check your paper **position**.
- **Pull** your downstrokes in the proper direction.
- **Shift** your paper as you write.

If you are left-handed . . .

Shift your paper as you write. Pull downstrokes toward your left elbow.

If you are right-handed . . .

Shift your paper as you write. Pull downstrokes toward the middle of your body.

Write the sentence. Check to see if your slant is uniform.

This is good slant.

Writing Lowercase Letters

To write legibly in cursive, you must form and join lowercase letters correctly.
The lessons in this unit will show you how.

 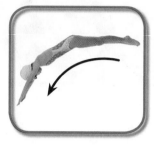  

As you write, you will focus on shape, size, spacing, and slant to help make your writing legible.

a　　*b*　　*c*　　*d*　　*e*　　*f*

g　　*h*　　*i*　　*j*　　*k*　　*l*

m　　*n*　　*o*　　*p*　　*q*　　*r*

s　　*t*　　*u*　　*v*　　*w*　　*x*

y　　*z*

Write the lowercase cursive alphabet.

18

Stop and Check

Circle your three best letters. Underline three letters you want to improve.

Beginning Strokes

The lowercase cursive letters are grouped by their beginning strokes.

Undercurve Letters

Trace undercurve strokes.

Trace letters that begin with an undercurve.

Downcurve Letters

Trace downcurve strokes.

Trace letters that begin with a downcurve.

Overcurve Letters

Trace overcurve strokes.

Trace letters that begin with an overcurve.

Before you join one letter to another, look at the way the letter ends.

Undercurve Ending

The letter i ends with an undercurve. Look at the ways i may be joined to other letters.

Joining i to:

Undercurve Beginning
$l \longrightarrow il$

Downcurve Beginning
$g \longrightarrow ig$

Overcurve Beginning
$n \longrightarrow in$

Write the joinings.

it   no   le   ry

Overcurve Ending

The letter g ends with an overcurve. Look at the ways g may be joined to other letters.

Joining g to:

Undercurve Beginning
$e \longrightarrow ge$

Downcurve Beginning
$a \longrightarrow ga$

Overcurve Beginning
$n \longrightarrow gn$

Write the joinings.

gy   je   zi   ya

Checkstroke Ending

The letter b ends with a checkstroke. Look at the ways b may be joined to other letters.

Joining b to:

Undercurve Beginning
$e \longrightarrow be$

Downcurve Beginning
$a \longrightarrow ba$

Overcurve Beginning
$y \longrightarrow by$

Write the joinings.

bi   ry   oa   wa

Write Undercurve Letters

Trace and write.

An undercurve begins each letter.

i   *i*   *i*   *i*   *i*   *i*   *i* ✓

t   *t*   *t*   *t*   *t*   *t*   *t* ✓

The letters *i* and *t* end with an undercurve. Write the joinings and words.

Undercurve-to-Undercurve	Undercurve-to-Downcurve	Undercurve-to-Overcurve
it *tw*	*id* *ta*	*in* *ty*
kite	*glide*	*wind*
twists	*tail*	*gusty*

Handwriting Tutor

Better *Letters*

Be careful not to loop back. Write:

i not *i*   *t* not *t*

Use your best handwriting to write the letters again.

Shape

Circle three letters you wrote that have good shape.

Write Undercurve Letters

Trace and write.

An undercurve begins each letter.

The letter _u_ ends with an undercurve. The letter _w_ ends with a checkstroke.
Write the joinings and the words.

Undercurve-to-Downcurve

ua ug

square

huge

Undercurve-to-Overcurve

um un

volume

pound

Checkstroke-to-Undercurve

we wi

weight

width

Handwriting Tutor

Better _Letters_

Be careful not to loop back. Write:
_u_ not _ee_   _w_ not _ie_

Use your best handwriting to write the letters again.

Stop and Check

Circle your best _u_ and your best _w_.

Trace and write.

An undercurve begins each letter.

_e_   e   e   e   e   e   e   e   e ✔

_l_   l   l   l   l   l   l   l   l ✔

The letters _e_ and _l_ end with an undercurve. Write the joinings and words.

Undercurve-to-Undercurve	**Undercurve-to-Downcurve**	**Undercurve-to-Overcurve**
er ls	ea lo	en ly
writer	read	send
e-mails	log on	quickly

Handwriting Tutor

Better _Letters_

Keep your loops open. Write:

e not ı   l not l

Use your best handwriting to write the letters again.

Size

Circle your best short letter and your best tall letter.

Write the words and the phrases.

inventions

screen   *start*   *link*

computer   *websites*

bulletin board   *laptop*

printer   *file*   *online*

Checkstroke Alert Join *w* and *r* at the midline. Write the joinings and the words.

wr   *wr*   *wr*   *wr*   *wr*

write   *wrist*   *wrap*

Write a paragraph about what you see in the picture.
Use words in the word bank. Be sure to leave space for margins.

hard drive
keyboard
monitor
mouse
mouse pad
power cord
printer
speakers

My writing has good Shape. ☐
My writing has good Size. ☐
My writing has good Spacing. ☐
My writing has good Slant. ☐

25

Write Undercurve Letters

Trace and write.

An undercurve begins each letter.

b   b   b   b   b   b   b   b ✓

h   h   h   h   h   h   h   h ✓

The letter *b* ends with a checkstroke. The letter *h* ends with an undercurve.
Write the joinings and the words.

Checkstroke-to-Undercurve	Checkstroke-to-Downcurve	Undercurve-to-Undercurve
bi br	ba bo	he hu
bike	bars	helmet
brakes	boxcar	hum

Handwriting Tutor

Better *Letters*

Keep your loops open. Write:

b not *b*   *h* not *h*

Use your best handwriting to write the letters again.

26

Stop and Check
Circle your best *b*
and your best *h*.

Trace and write.

An undercurve begins each letter.

f   f   f   f   f   f   f   f   f

k   k   k   k   k   k   k   k

The letters *f* and *k* end with an undercurve. Write the joinings and words.

Undercurve-to-Undercurve

fl   ks

flow

creeks

Undercurve-to-Downcurve

fo   ka

foam

kayak

Undercurve-to-Overcurve

fy   ky

leafy

risky

Handwriting Tutor

Better *Letters*

Keep your loops open. Write:

f not *f*   *k* not *k*

Use your best handwriting to write the letters again.

Spacing

Circle your best joining.

27

Write Undercurve Letters

Trace and write.

An undercurve begins each letter.

The letters *n* and *s* end with an undercurve. Write the joinings and words.

Undercurve-to-Undercurve	Undercurve-to-Downcurve	Undercurve-to-Overcurve
re su	*rg so*	*rn sy*
renew	*energy*	*return*
sun	*solar*	*system*

Handwriting Tutor

Better *Letters*

Be careful not to round *n* and *s*. Write:

n not *n*   *s* not *s*

Use your best handwriting to write the letters again.

Stop and Check

Circle your best *n* and your best *s*.

Trace and write.

An undercurve begins each letter.

j   j   j   j   j   j   j   j

p   p   p   p   p   p   p   p

The letter *j* ends with an overcurve. The letter *p* ends with an undercurve.
Write the joinings and the words.

Overcurve-to-Undercurve	**Undercurve-to-Undercurve**	**Undercurve-to-Downcurve**
ju je	pl pr	po pa
jury	explain	point
jest	process	pardon

Handwriting Tutor

Better Letters

Make sure to loop back. Write:

j not *j*   *p* not *p*

Use your best handwriting to write the letters again.

Slant

Circle a word you wrote that has good slant.

29

Write the words.

sail   *ship*   *mast*

chart   *plot a course*

explore   *rudder*   *keel*

forward   *aft*   *deck*

map   *jib*   *starboard*

Joining Alert

Remember! The undercurve-to-downcurve joining becomes a doublecurve. Write the joinings and the words.

pa   *sa*   *fa*   *package*

sash   *fast*

My writing has good **Shape**. ☐
My writing has good **Size**. ☐
My writing has good **Spacing**. ☐
My writing has good **Slant**. ☐

Write these sentences about water sports in cursive.
Then answer the question at the bottom of the page.

Gio went sailing.

Jack likes to go fishing.

Kijana loves swimming.

Aiko wants to scuba dive.

What is your favorite water sport? Write a short paragraph in cursive describing what you like to do on or in the water. Remember to indent the first line of the paragraph and leave space for margins.

Stop and Check

Circle your best letter.

31

Write Downcurve Letters

Trace and write.

A downcurve begins each letter.

a   *a   a   a   a   a   a   a*

d   *d   d   d   d   d   d   d*

The letters *a* and *d* end with an undercurve. Write the joinings and words.

Undercurve-to-Undercurve	Undercurve-to-Downcurve	Undercurve-to-Overcurve
ab di	*ac dd*	*an dy*
abacus	*facts*	*change*
divide	*add*	*study*

Handwriting Tutor

Better *Letters*

Close *a* and *d*. Write:
a not *u*   *d* not *d*

Use your best handwriting to write the letters again.

Stop and Check

Circle your best *a* and your best *d*.

Trace and write.

A downcurve begins each letter.

g   g   g   g   g   g   g   g

o   o   o   o   o   o   o   o

The letter _g_ ends with an overcurve. The letter _o_ ends with a checkstroke.
Write the joinings and words.

Overcurve-to-Undercurve	Checkstroke-to-Undercurve	Checkstroke-to-Overcurve
gr ge	ob ol	on oy
green	global	one
oxygen	ecology	enjoy

Handwriting Tutor

Better _Letters_

Be careful to close _g_ and _o_. Write:

_g_ not _y_   _o_ not _v_

Use your best handwriting to write the letters again.

Shape

Circle your three best letters that begin with a downcurve.

33

Write Downcurve Letters

Trace and write.

A downcurve begins each letter.

c c c c c c c c

q q q q q q q

The letters c and q end with an undercurve. Write the joinings and words.

Undercurve-to-Undercurve	Undercurve-to-Downcurve	Undercurve-to-Overcurve
qu qu	ca co	cy cn
quick	cartoon	bouncy
quip	comical	picnic

Handwriting Tutor

Better *Letters*

Be careful to close q. Write:

q not q

Use your best handwriting to write the letters again.

Stop and Check

Circle your best c and your best q.

34

Before you join one letter to another, look at the way the first letter ends.

Undercurve-to-Downcurve Joining

The undercurve swings wide and forms the top of the downcurve of the next letter.

la   do   to   ice   clay

Overcurve-to-Downcurve Joining

The overcurve crosses at the baseline, then continues up and wide to form the top of the downcurve letter.

ya   go   zo   jam   yawn

Checkstroke-to-Downcurve Joining

The checkstroke ending ⌣ swings right to form the top of the downcurve letter.

oo   bo   wa   bay   wool

Undercurve-to-Overcurve Joining

The undercurve swings wide and forms the top of the overcurve of the next letter.

nn   mm   na   funny   France

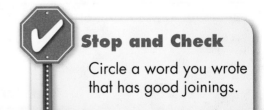

Stop and Check

Circle a word you wrote that has good joinings.

Write the words and phrases.

rain forest

forest floor   canopies

macaws   salamanders

quiet   humid   rain

towering   snakes

Checkstroke Alert! Join o with other letters at the midline. Write the joinings and words.

os   or   oo   ecosystem

orchid bloom

My writing has good *Shape* ☐
My writing has good *Size* ☐
My writing has good *Spacing* ☐
My writing has good *Slant* ☐

Write the paragraph about Amazon rain forest animals on the guidelines below. Use your best cursive, and remember to indent the first line and leave room for margins.

The Amazon rain forest is home to incredible animals. Toucans are beautiful birds with extremely long bills. Jaguars live on the rain forest floor, climb trees, and swim in water. And the anaconda might be the Amazon's most famous animal. It is the world's heaviest snake!

Stop and Check

Circle your best letter.

In the Real World

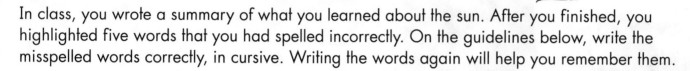
The more you practice writing in cursive, the easier it will be!

Learning cursive will help you write more quickly.
This can be important when taking notes in class.

In class, you wrote a summary of what you learned about the sun. After you finished, you highlighted five words that you had spelled incorrectly. On the guidelines below, write the misspelled words correctly, in cursive. Writing the words again will help you remember them.

> The sun is the center of our solar system. It is the closest star to Earth and gives Earth lite and heat. The sun's surface is made up of gas that is always muving. Prominences are clowds of gas that explode from the surface, and solar flares are qwite larger explosions. There are also cool, darc patches called sunspots.

Write Overcurve Letters

Trace and write.

An overcurve begins each letter.

n   n   n   n   n   n   n   n

m   m   m   m   m   m   m   m

The letters *n* and *m* end with an undercurve. Write the joinings and words.

Undercurve-to-Undercurve	Undercurve-to-Downcurve	Undercurve-to-Overcurve
nu me	nc ma	my nm
number	zinc	shiny
metal	magnet	column

Handwriting Tutor

Better *Letters*

Be careful to round *n* and *m*. Write:

n not *w*   *m* not *w*

Use your best handwriting to write the letters again.

Size

Circle your three best short letters.

39

Write Overcurve Letters

Trace and write.

An overcurve begins each letter.

y   *y*   *y*   *y*   *y*   *y*   *y*   *y* ✔

x   *x*   *x*   *x*   *x*   *x*   *x*   *x* ✔

The letter *y* ends with an overcurve. The letter *x* ends with an undercurve.
Write the joinings and words.

Overcurve-to-Undercurve	Overcurve-to-Overcurve	Undercurve-to-Undercurve
ye *ys*	*yn* *ym*	*xp* *xt*
year	*lynx*	*expect*
days	*symbol*	*next*

Handwriting Tutor

Better *Letters*

Be careful to round *y* and *x*. Write:

y not *y*   *x* not *x*

Use your best handwriting to write the letters again.

Stop and Check

Circle your best *y* and your best *x*.

40

Trace and write.

An overcurve begins each letter.

v   *v*   *v*   *v*   *v*   *v*   *v*   *v*

z   *z*   *z*   *z*   *z*   *z*   *z*   *z*

The letter *v* ends with a checkstroke. The letter *z* ends with an overcurve.
Write the joinings and words.

Checkstroke-to-Downcurve	**Overcurve-to-Undercurve**	**Overcurve-to-Downcurve**
va *vo*	*ze* *zi*	*za* *zo*
lava	*haze*	*hazard*
volcano	*zigzag*	*zoom*

Handwriting Tutor

Better *Letters*

Be careful to round *v* and *z*. Write:
v not *v*   *z* not *z*

Use your best handwriting to write the letters again.

Spacing

Circle a word you wrote that has good joinings.

41

Write the words.

animals

ox   viper   fox

chimpanzee   buzzard

yak   hyena   turkey

zebra   zoo   vulture

Checkstroke Alert Each word has a checkstroke joining at the midline. Write the words.

mouse   ostrich   boar

lion   oxen

My writing has good Shape. ☐
My writing has good Size. ☐
My writing has good Spacing. ☐
My writing has good Slant. ☐

Look at the photo below, and read the lists of nouns and adjectives. Circle the three nouns and the three adjectives that you think fit the photo.

Nouns	Adjectives
chimpanzees	asleep
gorillas	excited
hands	five
jungle	hairy
zebras	alert
zoo	two

Write a short paragraph in cursive describing the photo. Use the six words you circled. Remember to indent the first line of your paragraph and leave space for margins.

Stop and Check

Circle your best letter.

43

Keys to Legibility

Slant
Spacing
Size
Shape

Write the steps for washing a dog.
Make your writing easy to read.

1. get dog wet

2. wash with shampoo

3. rinse with water

4. brush and dry

44

Write the steps for a task you know how to do. Be sure to leave space for margins.

Is your writing easy to read?

Shape Circle your best letter that has an undercurve beginning.

Spacing Circle two words that have space for \ between them.

Size Circle your best short letter.

Slant Circle a word you wrote that has good slant.

Lowercase Review

Write undercurve letters.

i t u w e l b

h f k r s j p

Write downcurve letters.

a d g o c q

Write overcurve letters.

n m y x v z

Circle your best letter in each group above. Write the letters you want to improve.

Write the joinings.

it ea ry ye ga wr bo

Manuscript Maintenance

Bicycle Parts

seat

grip

handlebars

rear reflector

crossbar

front reflector

seat post

brake line   tire

reflector

rim

gears

spoke

spoke   chain   pedal   wheel   reflector

Unscramble the name of each bicycle part. Write the names in manuscript.

badlehanrs _____

atse _____

irpg _____

atse sopt _____

ehewl _____

ossrcarb _____

riet _____

deapl _____

mir _____

toreclfer _____

skope _____

ihcna _____

Cursive Numerals

1 2 3 4 5
6 7 8 9 10

Write the missing numerals.

14, 16, 18, _____, _____, 24, _____

Write the missing numerals.

78, 79, _____, _____, 82, 83, _____

Write the odd numbers between 1 and 13.

1, _____, _____, _____, _____, _____, 13

Write the even numbers between 10 and 20.

10, _____, _____, _____, _____, 20

Here are two magic squares. The sum of the numbers in a magic square's rows and columns is always the same. Fill in the missing numerals.

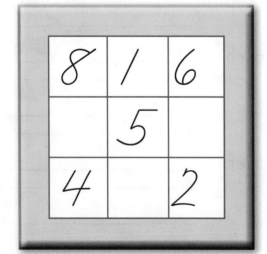

8	1	6
	5	
4		2

1		14	4
12	6	7	
	10	11	
13		2	16

48

Write these facts about time in your best cursive handwriting.

A minute is 60 seconds.

An hour is 60 minutes.

A day is 24 hours.

A week is 7 days.

A year is 12 months.

A year is 365 days.

A leap year is 366 days.

A decade is 10 years.

Writing Uppercase Letters

To write legibly in cursive, you must write uppercase letters well. In the lessons in this unit, the uppercase letters are grouped by common strokes. You will learn when and when not to join an uppercase letter to the letter that follows.

As you write, you will focus on shape, size, spacing, and slant to help make your writing legible.

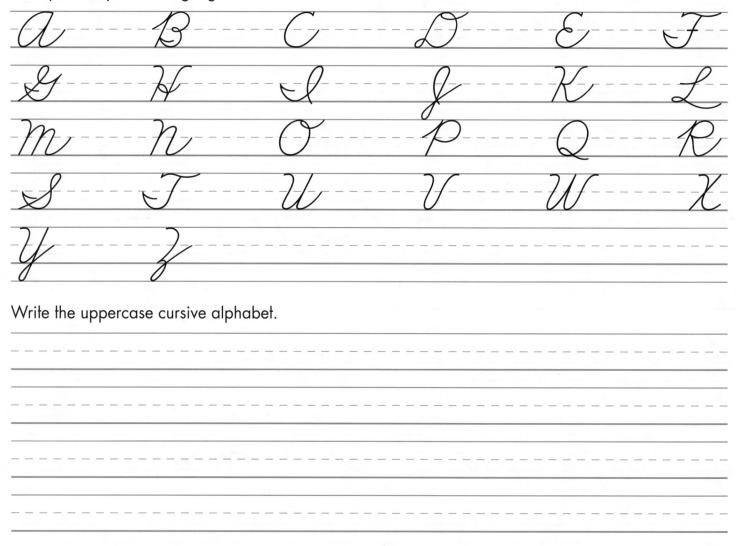

Write the uppercase cursive alphabet.

Circle your three best letters. Underline three letters you want to improve.

Beginning Strokes

The uppercase letters are grouped by their strokes.

Downcurve Letters

Trace downcurve strokes and letters.

Curve Forward Letters

Trace curve forward-slant strokes and curve forward letters.

Overcurve and Doublecurve Letters

Trace overcurve strokes and letters.

Trace doublecurve strokes and letters.

Undercurve-Loop and Undercurve-Slant Letters

Trace undercurve-loop strokes and letters.

Trace undercurve-slant strokes and letters.

Write Downcurve Letters

Trace and write.

A downcurve begins each letter.

𝒶   𝒶 𝒶 𝒶 𝒶 𝒶 𝒶 𝒶

𝒪   𝒪 𝒪 𝒪 𝒪 𝒪 𝒪 𝒪

Joining Alert   𝒶 is joined to the letter that follows, but 𝒪 is not.

Write the words and sentences.

Alabama   Oklahoma

America is beautiful.

Our flag flies proudly.

Handwriting Tutor

Better *Letters*

Make sure to close 𝒶 and 𝒪. Write:
𝒶 not 𝒶   𝒪 not 𝒪

Use your best handwriting to write the letters again.

Stop and Check

Circle your best joining.

52

Trace and write.

Find a downcurve in each letter.

$\mathcal{D}$ $\mathcal{D}$ $\mathcal{D}$ $\mathcal{D}$ $\mathcal{D}$ $\mathcal{D}$ $\mathcal{D}$

$\mathcal{C}$ $\mathcal{C}$ $\mathcal{C}$ $\mathcal{C}$ $\mathcal{C}$ $\mathcal{C}$ $\mathcal{C}$

Joining Alert $\mathcal{C}$ is joined to the letter that follows, but $\mathcal{D}$ is not.

Write the words and sentences.

David   *Deb*   *Cam*   *Cara*

Dan speaks Chinese.

Chinese is fun to learn.

Handwriting Tutor

Better Letters

Close $\mathcal{D}$. Make sure $\mathcal{C}$ has good slant. Write:

$\mathcal{D}$ not $\mathcal{D}$ $\mathcal{C}$ not $\mathcal{C}$

Use your best handwriting to write the letters again.

Slant

Circle a word you wrote that has good slant.

53

Write Downcurve Letters

Trace and write.

Find a downcurve in $\mathcal{E}$.

$\mathcal{E}$ $\mathcal{E}$ $\mathcal{E}$ $\mathcal{E}$ $\mathcal{E}$ $\mathcal{E}$ $\mathcal{E}$ $\mathcal{E}$

Joining Alert $\mathcal{E}$ is joined to the letter that follows.

Write the words and sentences.

Encino   Erie   Elkhart

Eddie   Eve   Evan   Elly

Eve spied an eagle's nest.

Eaglets are baby eagles.

Handwriting Tutor

Better *Letters*

Make a loop in $\mathcal{E}$. Write:
$\mathcal{E}$ not $\mathcal{E}$

Use your best handwriting to write the letters again.

54

Stop and Check

Circle your best joining.

Joining *a*, *c*, and *e*

a, *c*, and *e* are joined to the letter that follows. The undercurve swings up to the midline to form the first curve of the next letter. The joining must be wide enough to allow room for joining to the next letter.

Write the words and sentence.

Adam   Abby   Ajay   Ann

Cory   Chloe   Cam   Clay

Eva   Eric   Emma   Ethan

Eve spied an eagle's nest.

The cursive letters *a*, *c*, and *e* are joined to the letter that follows.

Stop and Check

Circle your best joining.

55

Write the names of desert places.

El Paso, Texas

Oraibi, Arizona

Death Valley, California

Deserts are dry places. Cactus plants live there. Only a few animals do. After rain, a desert blooms.

Write the paragraph. Remember to begin each sentence with an uppercase letter.

My writing has good **Shape**. ☐
My writing has good **Size**. ☐
My writing has good **Spacing**. ☐
My writing has good **Slant**. ☐

Road Trip

Plan a road trip across the country, starting in an eastern state along the Atlantic Ocean and finishing in a western state along the Pacific Ocean. Choose five cities you will visit, including your starting and ending city.

Here's your challenge: Choose cities that begin with each of these uppercase letters: a, C, D, E, and O.

Write a short paragraph on the guidelines below. Tell which city you will start in, which city you'll end in, and which three cities you'll visit in between. Remember to leave space for margins.

My Road Trip Plan

The more you practice writing in cursive, the easier it will be!

In the Real World

Learning cursive will help you write more quickly.
This can be important when writing a personal schedule.

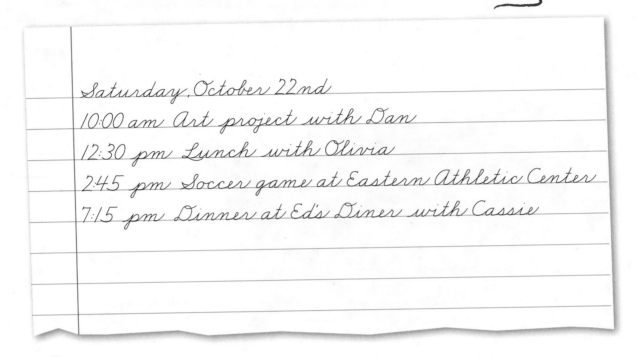

Saturday, October 22nd
10:00 am Art project with Dan
12:30 pm Lunch with Olivia
2:45 pm Soccer game at Eastern Athletic Center
7:15 pm Dinner at Ed's Diner with Cassie

Write the schedule.

Write Curve Forward Letters

Trace and write.

Both n and m begin with a curve forward stroke.

n n n n n n n ✓

m m m m m m m ✓

Joining Alert n and m are joined to the letter that follows.

Write the words and sentences.

Nevada   Maryland   Maine

Nell went to Montana.

Mountain hikes were fun.

Handwriting Tutor

Better Letters

Start m and n just under the headline. Write:
m not m n not n

Use your best handwriting to write the letters again.

Shape

Circle your three best letters with an undercurve ending.

59

Write Curve Forward Letters

Trace and write.

Find a curve forward stroke in each letter.

H *H* *H* *H* *H* *H* *H*

K *K* *K* *K* *K* *K* *K*

Joining Alert *H* and *K* are joined to the letter that follows.

Write the words and sentences.

Hawaii   Kahului   Kauai

Kate likes Honolulu.

Her dad saw orchids there.

Handwriting Tutor

Better *Letters*

Lift after the first stroke for *H* and *K*. Write:

H not *H*   *K* not *K*

Use your best handwriting to write the letters again.

Stop and Check
Circle your best *H*
and your best *K*.

Trace and write.

Find a curve forward stroke in each letter.

U U U U U U U U

Y Y Y Y Y Y Y Y

Joining Alert 𝒰 and 𝒴 are joined to the letter that follows.

Write the words and sentences.

Utah   New York   Yuma

The United States is vast.

You and I live there.

Handwriting Tutor

Better Letters

Start 𝒰 and 𝒴 with a curve forward stroke. Write:

𝒰 not 𝒰   𝒴 not 𝒴

Use your best handwriting to write the letters again.

Size

Circle your three best letters that have a descender.

Write the names of Native American peoples.

Hopi Yamasee

Kickapoo Natchez Navajo

Huron Maya Yuma Ute

Navajo art is beautiful. Museums have some of it. Young artists make rings. How lovely they are!

Write the paragraph about Navajo art. Remember to begin each sentence with an uppercase letter.

My writing has good Shape. ☐
My writing has good Size. ☐
My writing has good Spacing. ☐
My writing has good Slant. ☐

Read the beginning of the story to the right.

Yuli was from New Mexico, and Heather was from Kansas. The two girls became friends at camp in Utah. One summer, the most exciting thing happened when they went hiking in the Grand Canyon.

On the guidelines below, finish the story by writing what you think happened next. Write in cursive, and remember to leave room for margins.

Stop and Check

Circle your best letter.

63

Write Curve Forward Letters

Trace and write.

Find a curve forward stroke in each letter.

$\mathcal{Z}$ is joined to the letter that follows, but $\mathcal{V}$ is not.

Write the words and sentences.

Zoe   Zelda   Victor   Vera

Violins have four strings.

Zithers have strings also.

Handwriting Tutor

Better *Letters*

Start $\mathcal{Z}$ and $\mathcal{V}$ with a curve forward stroke.
Write: $\mathcal{Z}$ not $\mathcal{Z}$ $\mathcal{V}$ not V

Use your best handwriting to write the letters again.

Stop and Check

Circle your best $\mathcal{Z}$ and your best $\mathcal{V}$.

64

Trace and write.

A curve forward begins each letter.

W   W   W   W   W   W   W   W

X   X   X   X   X   X   X   X

Joining Alert! W and X are not joined to the letter that follows.

Write the words and sentences.

Will   Wendy   Xavier

What are X-rays?

X-rays are beams of light.

Handwriting Tutor

Better Letters

Start W and X with a curve forward stroke.
Write: W not W   X not X

Use your best handwriting to write the letters again.

Spacing

Circle your best spacing between letters that are not joined.

Write the names of inventors.

Vladimir Zworykin

George Washington Carver

Wilbur and Orville Wright

Wheels turn on axles.
X-rays show bones.
Zippers fasten jackets.
Velcro holds things together.

Write the sentences about inventions. Begin each sentence with an uppercase letter.
Leave room for margins.

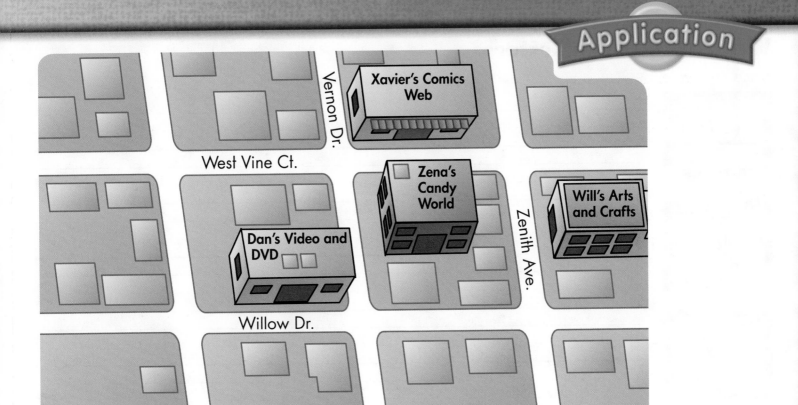

Look at the town center map above to plan a day of shopping.
You need to buy the following items in this order:

1. a box of chocolates
2. a comic book
3. a set of watercolor paints
4. a DVD movie

On the guidelines below, write the stores and the street names you need to visit in the proper order.
Use your best cursive handwriting.

Write Overcurve Letters

Trace and write.

Find an overcurve in each letter.

I *I* *I* *I* *I* *I* *I*

J *J* *J* *J* *J* *J* *J*

Q *Q* *Q* *Q* *Q* *Q* *Q*

Joining Alert! *J* is joined to the letter that follows, but *I* and *Q* are not.

Write the names.

Inez *Justin* *Quinn*

Isabella *Jackie* *Quincy*

Handwriting Tutor

Better *Letters*

Write: *I* not *I* , *J* not *J* , *Q* not *Q*

Use your best handwriting to write the letters again.

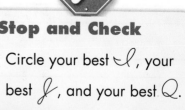

Stop and Check

Circle your best *I*, your best *J*, and your best *Q*.

Write Doublecurve Letters

Trace and write.

There is a doublecurve in each letter.

𝒯 𝒯 𝒯 𝒯 𝒯 𝒯 𝒯 𝒯

✓

𝒻 𝒻 𝒻 𝒻 𝒻 𝒻 𝒻 𝒻

✓

Joining Alert! 𝒯 and 𝒻 are not joined to the letter that follows.

Write the names and sentences.

Tara Tim Fiona Finn

Forests keep us healthy.

Their leaves make oxygen.

Handwriting Tutor

Better Letters

Lift after the curve forward and right stroke.
Write: 𝒯 not 𝒯   𝒻 not 𝒻

Use your best handwriting to write the letters again.

Slant

Circle three words you wrote that have good slant.

69

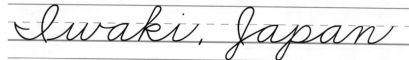

Write the names of coastal cities.

Iwaki, Japan

Tocopilla, Chile

Qingdao, China

Tsunamis are huge waves. Floods come if one hits. I saw one once on television. Japan has tsunamis.

Write the paragraph. Begin each sentence with an uppercase letter. Leave room for margins.

Listed below are some famous landmarks and their locations.

Niagara Falls: New York   Mount Rushmore: South Dakota
Hoover Dam: Nevada   Kennedy Space Center: Florida
United States Capitol: Washington, D.C.   Yosemite National Park: California

Write the name of the famous place you would see in each city or state. Use your best cursive writing.

Visit South Dakota to see

Visit New York to see

Visit California to see

Visit Washington, D.C., to see

Visit Nevada to see

Visit Florida to see

Write Undercurve-Loop Letters

Trace and write.

Find an undercurve-loop in each letter.

G G G G G G G

S S S S S S S

L L L L L L L

Joining Alert! G, S, and L are not joined to the letter that follows.

Write the names of landmarks.

The Statue of Liberty

The Golden Gate Bridge

Handwriting Tutor

Better Letters

Remember to keep loops open.
Write: G not G , S not S , L not L

Use your best handwriting to write the letters again.

Stop and Check

Circle your best G, your best S, and your best L.

Write Undercurve-Slant Letters

Trace and write.

Find an undercurve-slant in each letter.

P   P   P   P   P   P   P   P   P ✓

R   R   R   R   R   R   R   R   R ✓

B   B   B   B   B   B   B   B   B ✓

Joining Alert! R is joined to the letter that follows, but P and B are not.

Write the names of cities.

Phoenix   Raleigh   Buffalo

Boulder   Philadelphia

Handwriting Tutor

Better Letters

Begin with an undercurve stroke.
Write: P not P , R not R , B not B

Use your best handwriting to write the letters again.

Shape

Circle your three best letters with an undercurve beginning.

Write the names of baseball teams.

Boston Red Sox

Pittsburgh Pirates

San Francisco Giants

Pieces of equipment for playing baseball:
1. Baseball 2. Bat 3. Glove
4. Helmet 5. Shin Guards

Write the note about baseball equipment.

This timeline is out of order. Write the dates and events in the proper order below. Use your best cursive handwriting.

Professional Baseball Timeline

1903	1947	1876	1974	1900	1935
Boston and Pittsburgh play first World Series.	Jackie Robinson is first African American in majors.	National League is formed.	Hank Aaron breaks Babe Ruth's home run record.	American League is formed.	George Herman "Babe" Ruth hits final home run.

My favorite team is the Green Bay Packers. My brother Levi likes the Saint Louis Rams. My sister Gwen doesn't agree with either of us. She is a Chicago Bears fan. But we all think that football is the best sport ever!

Write the paragraph about football teams.
Make your writing easy to read. Be sure to leave space for margins.

Is your writing easy to read?

Shape
Circle your best letter that has an undercurve-loop beginning.

Spacing
Circle two words that have space for \ between them.

Size
Circle your best tall letter.

Slant
Circle a word you wrote that has good slant.

Uppercase Review

Write downcurve letters.

A O D C E

Write curve forward letters.

N M H K U Y Z V W X

Write overcurve letters.

I J Q

Write doublecurve letters.

T F

Write undercurve-loop letters.

G S L

Write undercurve-slant letters.

P R B

Write the names of cities.

Ithaca Tulsa Seattle

Baltimore Dallas Xenia

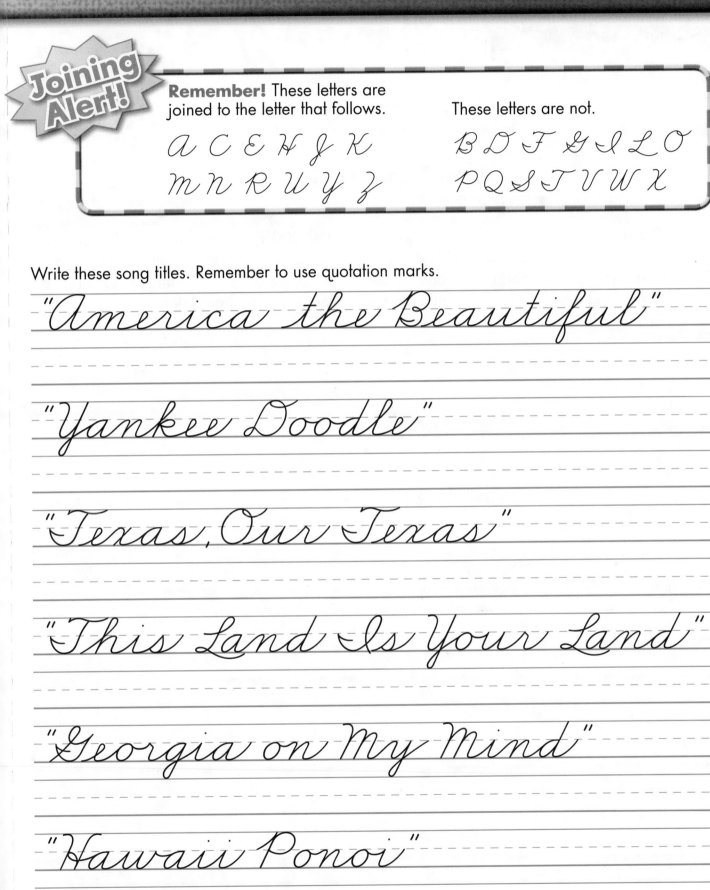

Remember! These letters are joined to the letter that follows.

A C E H J K M N R U Y Z

These letters are not.

B D F G I L O P Q S T V W X

Write these song titles. Remember to use quotation marks.

"America the Beautiful"

"Yankee Doodle"

"Texas, Our Texas"

"This Land Is Your Land"

"Georgia on My Mind"

"Hawaii Ponoi"

Make a Flow Chart

A Flow Chart shows steps in a process. This chart shows how steel is made from iron ore. Use manuscript to write the steps in order in the Flow Chart. Make your writing fit the space.

Iron Into Steel

4	7	1	6	3	5	2
Oxygen is mixed into the liquid iron.	The steel is made into cars, bridges, trains, and buildings.	Iron ore is mined out of the earth.	The liquid steel cools and hardens into blocks.	At 3,000°F, the iron becomes liquid.	The iron and oxygen change into liquid steel.	The ore is put into a hot furnace.

1.

2.

3.

4.

5.

6.

7.

Journal Entry

Sometimes you write just for yourself. When you write for yourself, you don't have to be as neat as when you write for someone else. But your writing must still be legible. You should be able to read what you have written now and at some future time, too.

For example, you might write a journal entry that is for your eyes only. In the space below, write a journal entry that tells what you did yesterday. Leave space for margins.

Date:

The more you practice writing in cursive, the easier it will be. On the following pages, you will write for yourself by making a schedule and taking notes. You will write in a new, smaller size, too. You will focus on the four Keys to Legibility to help make your writing easy to read.

Schedule

Writing a schedule can help you remember things you must do and places you must be. It can also help you remember the order in which you will do things. Here is a schedule:

Monday	4:00	*basketball practice in gym*
	5:00	*help Mom wash Rover*
Tuesday	3:00	*Service Club meeting*
Wednesday		

Add these items to the schedule:

| Tuesday | 8:00 | *surprise party for Grandma* |
| Wednesday | 7:00 | *social studies project with Judy, Kamal, and T'Aysha* |

Make sure that your tall letters do not bump into the descenders above them.

| Are your short letters half the height of your tall letters? | Yes | No |
| Do your letters have good shape? | Yes | No |

Use cursive to write a schedule of things you might do next week.
Pay attention to the size of your letters.

Monday

Tuesday

Wednesday

Thursday

Friday

Saturday

Are your short letters half the height of your tall letters?   Yes   No

Notes

When you take notes from a book, write the title and the author.
Then write the important facts in your own words.

Flight! by Harry Roberts
1804— Sir George Cayley builds and
           flies first successful glider
1896— Samuel P. Langley flies model of
           a steam-powered airplane over
           Potomac River
1900–1903— Orville and Wilbur Wright
           build and test glider

Write the notes. Try to write quickly, but make sure your writing is still legible.

My writing has good Shape. ☐
My writing has good Size. ☐
My writing has good Spacing. ☐
My writing has good Slant. ☐

Take notes from the following paragraph.
Make your writing easy to read.

Flight! by Harry Roberts

On December 17, 1903, Orville and Wilbur Wright flew their plane in Kitty Hawk, North Carolina, four times. The soil was sandy and soft so they would not get badly hurt if they crashed. The first flight was 12 seconds long. The fourth flight covered 852 feet in 59 seconds. The Wright brothers had made history. They were the first people to fly a heavier-than-air machine with an engine.

Title and author:

Who flew?

Where?

When?

Why are the Wright brothers famous?

Are all your tall letters the same size?　　Yes　No

Phone Message

Sometimes you write things for someone else to read. When you write for someone else, you must be sure that your writing is legible.

Juan took this phone message for his sister.

What makes Juan's message legible?
Check each true statement.

☐ There is space for O between letters.

☐ There is space for \ between words.

☐ There is space for O between sentences.

Add this message to the pad.

P. S. Call 555-1235 if you can't make it. She'll be in the office until 5:00.

Thursday

Maria,
Sophia Martin called at 10:00. Your job interview at J.P. Insurance Company will be on Monday at 4:00. Good luck!
Juan

On the following pages, you will write a friendly letter, a school paper, an invitation, and a thank-you note. As you write, you will focus on spacing to help make your writing legible.

Friendly Letter

Read this friendly letter. Notice its five parts.

> 581 Ashley Court
> Hickory, North Carolina 28601   ← heading
> March 5, 20 ____
>
> Dear Brittany,   ← greeting
>
>   Great news! I got a puppy! I named her
> Button because she is small and round. She
> has fluffy brown fur and cute little ears.   ← body
>   I heard you made the track team. Good work!
>
>   Your friend,   ← closing
>   Nica   ← signature

Write the body of a letter to a friend. Pay attention to the spacing between letters, words, and sentences. You can copy the one above, or you can write your own.

Spacing

Is there proper spacing between letters?	Yes	No
Is there proper spacing between words?	Yes	No
Is there proper spacing between sentences?	Yes	No

Headings

When you write for school, you usually write a heading and a title on your paper. The heading might contain your name, your teacher's name, the subject, and the date.

Write the paragraph to complete Taylor's paper.

Our class should visit the aquarium. We can get there by bus. We could see the giant saltwater tank. We might see the sharks being fed.

Taylor Sheets
Mrs. Johnson
Science
April 17
　　　　My Idea for a Class Trip

My writing has good Shape. ❑
My writing has good Size. ❑
My writing has good Spacing. ❑
My writing has good Slant. ❑

Complete the heading on this paper. Then write a paragraph about a trip that your class could take. Give at least three reasons why the class should take this trip.

Name:

Teacher:

Subject:

Date:

Title:

Invitation

Use your best handwriting when you write an invitation. Use this information to fill out the party invitation below.

- *The party is for Andrea.*
- *The date is May 25.*
- *The time is 1:00.*
- *The address is   62 Sunset Avenue*
  Wichita Falls, Texas
- *RSVP by May 15 to 555-7716.*

For:

Date:

Time:

Place:

RSVP:

Thank-You Note

Here is a thank-you note that Andrea wrote after her party.

June 5

Dear Matt,

Thank you for helping me decorate the yard for my party. There was so much to do! The yard looked great. Thank you again.

Your friend,
Andrea

Write Andrea's thank-you note to Matt, or write a note to thank someone who has helped you.

My writing has good Shape. ☐
My writing has good Size. ☐
My writing has good Spacing. ☐
My writing has good Slant. ☐

Handwriting and the Writing Process

News Story

A news story is a factual report about a current event. It uses facts to tell about the event. A news story does not tell the writer's opinion.

Follow these steps for writing a news story.

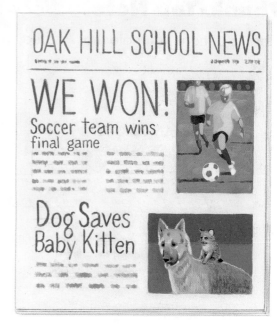

I. Prewriting

Start by thinking about a topic for your news story. Imagine that your readers will be the students in your class. **Brainstorm** topics to add to the list below. Write legibly so you can read your ideas later.

school team wins a big game

class visitors

new student in class

school concert

new class pet

school play opens

Look back at your list. Choose your topic. Write the subject of your news story below.

Answer the "5W's and H" questions to plan your news story.

What happened?

Who was involved?

When did it happen?

Where did it happen?

Why did it happen?

How did it happen?

News stories start with the most important facts and end with the least important. List facts for your news story from most important to least important.

Most important

Least important

2. Drafting

Write your first draft. Begin your news story with a sentence that will get your readers' attention.

Slant

Is your writing legible?	Yes	No
Did you position your paper correctly?	Yes	No
Does your writing have uniform slant?	Yes	No

3. Revising

Read your draft and mark any changes you want to make. You may want to ask a classmate to help you. Use the editing marks below as you revise your news story.

≡ Make a capital.

╱ Use lowercase.

⊙ Add a period.

∧ Insert or add.

Delete or take out.

Indent for a new paragraph.

4. Editing

Check your news story for errors in spelling, punctuation, and capitalization. Then answer the questions below to help you check your handwriting. You may want to ask a classmate to help you.

Do your letters have good shape?	Yes	No
Are all your tall letters the same size?	Yes	No
Are your short letters half the size of your tall letters?	Yes	No
Did you avoid collisions?	Yes	No
Is there space for O between letters?	Yes	No
Is there space for ╲ between words?	Yes	No
Is there space for $\mathcal{O}$ between sentences?	Yes	No
Does your writing have uniform slant?	Yes	No
Is your writing legible?	Yes	No

5. Publishing

Use your best handwriting to make a final copy of your news story. Then follow these steps to publish your news story:

- Add a title.
- Add your name as a byline.
- Add an illustration, if you wish.
- Post your story on a bulletin board with everyone else's stories.
- Read the class newspaper!

Math or Science?

Which content area do you enjoy more: math or science? Write your opinion and at least two supporting reasons. Be sure to include facts and details. Remember to indent the first line of each paragraph you write and to leave space for margins.

Problem Solving

Write a short story about a time you had a problem, and explain how you solved it. Use transitional words (such as *next, then, after*) and phrases to manage the sequence of events. Be sure to include sensory details to make your writing precise. End your writing with a conclusion. Remember to indent the first line of each paragraph you write and to leave space for margins.

Response to Literature

Write the title of a book you have read. Then write your opinion about the book. Use words and phrases to link your opinion to reasons. Be sure to include a concluding statement. Underline the title of your book. Remember to indent the first line of each paragraph you write and to leave space for margins.

Title:

Social Studies Essay

Write a short informative/explanatory essay about a social studies topic you are learning about in class. Be sure to develop your topic with facts, definitions, and examples. Provide a concluding statement related to the information you presented. Remember to indent the first line of each paragraph you write and to leave space for margins.

Handwriting and the Writing Process
Write a Paragraph

A paragraph is a group of sentences about one subject.
Use the steps below to write a paragraph about how to play
your favorite game.

1. Prewriting

Prewriting means gathering ideas and planning before you write.
List your ideas on a piece of paper. Then plan your paragraph,
telling the subject and in what order you will write your ideas.

2. Drafting

Drafting means putting your thoughts into written sentences for the
first time. Use the ideas you listed in Prewriting to draft your paragraph.
Write your first draft.

3. Revising

Revising means changing your writing to make it say exactly what
you mean. Read your draft. Mark any changes you want to make.

Does your writing include all the information readers want to know?	Yes No
Does your writing include descriptive details?	Yes No

4. Editing

Editing means checking your revised writing for errors in spelling,
punctuation, capitalization, and handwriting.

Are all words spelled correctly?	Yes No
Have you used uppercase letters and punctuation correctly?	Yes No
Do your letters have good shape and size?	Yes No
Is there good spacing between letters, words, and sentences?	Yes No
Does your writing have uniform slant?	Yes No
Is your writing easy to read?	Yes No

5. Publishing

Publishing means using your best handwriting to make an error-free
copy of your writing. Share your writing.

Writing Quickly

Writing quickly is a skill that you need to draft a story, write a timed test, or take notes as your teacher talks. Writing that is done quickly should still be easy to read. With practice, you will learn how to make your writing speedy and legible.

Read the lines of poetry below. They are part of a poem written by Julia A. Fletcher Carney in 1845. Write the poem quickly and legibly.

Little drops of water,
Little grains of sand,
Make the mighty ocean
And the pleasant land.

Write the lines of poetry again. Try to write even faster, but make sure your writing is still legible.

Write the lines of poetry two more times. Try to write even faster, but keep your writing easy to read.

_____

_____

_____

_____

_____

_____

_____

_____

_____

_____

Now read your final writing. Circle Yes or No to respond to each statement. Then show your writing to another reader, either a classmate or your teacher. Ask that person to circle Yes or No beside each statement.

	My Evaluation		My Classmate's or Teacher's Evaluation	
The writing is easy to read.	Yes	No	Yes	No
The writing has good Shape.	Yes	No	Yes	No
The writing has good Size.	Yes	No	Yes	No
The writing has good Spacing.	Yes	No	Yes	No
The writing has good Slant.	Yes	No	Yes	No

Writing Easily

As you write stories and essays for school papers and tests, it is important that your handwriting flows easily. When you automatically know how to write legibly, you don't have to worry about your handwriting. You are free to think about what you want your writing to say. With practice, you will learn how to make your writing easy, quick, and legible.

Read the writing prompt below. Respond to it by writing on the lines. Let your handwriting flow easily as you think and write. Remember to indent your paragraphs and to leave space for margins.

Think about something interesting you have seen.

Write a description of what you saw.
Include details to help the reader see
what you are describing.

Now read your final writing. Circle Yes or No to respond to each statement. Then show your writing to another reader, either a classmate or your teacher. Ask that person to circle Yes or No beside each statement.

	My Evaluation		My Classmate's or Teacher's Evaluation	
The writing is easy to read.	Yes	No	Yes	No
The writing has good **Shape**.	Yes	No	Yes	No
The writing has good **Size**.	Yes	No	Yes	No
The writing has good **Spacing**.	Yes	No	Yes	No
The writing has good **Slant**.	Yes	No	Yes	No

It's Dark in Here

I am writing these poems
From inside a lion,
And it's rather dark in here.
So please excuse the handwriting
Which may not be too clear.
But this afternoon by the lion's cage
I'm afraid I got too near.
And I'm writing these lines
From inside a lion,
And it's rather dark in here.

by Shel Silverstein

Write the poem in your best cursive handwriting. Leave space for margins.

Is your writing easy to read?   Yes   No

Write your five best cursive letters.

Write five cursive letters you would like to improve.

Write the Sentence

The quick brown fox jumps over the lazy dog.

The quick brown fox jumps over the lazy dog.

Record of Student's Handwriting Skills
Cursive

	Needs Improvement	Shows Mastery
Sits correctly	❑	❑
Holds pencil correctly	❑	❑
Positions paper correctly	❑	❑
Writes numerals /–10	❑	❑
Writes undercurve letters: *i, t, u, w, e, l*	❑	❑
Writes undercurve letters: *b, h, f, k, r, s, j, p*	❑	❑
Writes downcurve letters: *a, d, g, o, c, q*	❑	❑
Writes overcurve letters: *n, m, y, x, v, z*	❑	❑
Writes downcurve letters: *A, O, D, C, E*	❑	❑
Writes curve forward letters: *N, M, H, K, U, Y*	❑	❑
Writes curve forward letters: *Z, V, W, X*	❑	❑
Writes overcurve letters: *I, J, Q*	❑	❑
Writes doublecurve letters: *T, F*	❑	❑
Writes undercurve-loop letters: *G, S, L*	❑	❑
Writes undercurve-slant letters: *P, R, B*	❑	❑
Writes the undercurve-to-undercurve joining	❑	❑

	Needs Improvement	Shows Mastery
Writes the undercurve-to-downcurve joining	❑	❑
Writes the undercurve-to-overcurve joining	❑	❑
Writes the overcurve-to-undercurve joining	❑	❑
Writes the overcurve-to-downcurve joining	❑	❑
Writes the overcurve-to-overcurve joining	❑	❑
Writes the checkstroke-to-undercurve joining	❑	❑
Writes the checkstroke-to-downcurve joining	❑	❑
Writes the checkstroke-to-overcurve joining	❑	❑
Writes in the new size	❑	❑
Writes with correct shape	❑	❑
Writes with correct size	❑	❑
Writes with correct spacing	❑	❑
Writes with uniform slant	❑	❑
Writes legibly for self	❑	❑
Writes legibly for someone else	❑	❑
Writes legibly for publication	❑	❑
Regularly checks written work for legibility	❑	❑

Index